Astronomical Learning

Astronomical Tutor

Published by Astronomical Tutor, 2024.

While every precaution has been taken in the preparation of this book, the publisher assumes no responsibility for errors or omissions, or for damages resulting from the use of the information contained herein.

ASTRONOMICAL LEARNING

First edition. May 1, 2024.

Copyright © 2024 Astronomical Tutor.

ISBN: 979-8224754526

Written by Astronomical Tutor.

Table of Contents

I dedicate this book to the public school system that challenged my children. While it may have tested our resolve, it also ignited a determination within my family to defy the odds. Through this struggle, we forged a neurodiversity-affirming and strength-based approach that empowered my kids to flourish, anchored by structured literacy and math in out independent home-school.

If you have purchased this book I hope you are invested and interested in improving the future of education for the better. I hope that like myself you have been shocked by reports of abuse, illiteracy, chronic absenteeism, and discrimination internationally around the world of education.

My introduction to this issue came personally to my family when in 2021 my own daughter was subject to this all too common experience of discrimination. It started when she was four years old in preschool enrolled in a local public elementary school. She is my husband and I's first born child. We thought we did everything right. My husband and I both attended local brick and mortar public schools our entire educational career. We both graduated from highschool with a diploma. We both ended up going to college afterwards. Sadly both of us had working parents and had to take out student loans. We both cut our college education short in order to support our own adult lives. We got full time jobs.

When we made the decision to become parents we knew we had learned most of our life skills within the thick cemented walls of a public school. Nothing was ever indicated to us that it would not become the same future for our own children. In 2020, the covid-19 pandemic was happening. I was a stay at home mom. I decided to make it my responsibility as a mother to foster my daughter's "love of learning". Early on she was very excited. She already knew the alphabet and counted to 40 on her own by the age of two. At every well check pediatrician appointment she would get compliments on her intelligence.

I was excited that spring in 2020 to find out all of the details about signing my daughter up for preschool. We had no hesitation from the pediatrician, family members, or ourselves that starting school at the age of four wouldn't be successful. I was still going to be a stay at home mother to my young son so I knew if I had to pick up my daughter at any time of the day it would not be an issue.

My husband and I had met the preschool teacher, we did the school walk through, and our daughter was excited to expand on the knowledge she already knew. School started August 2021. It was almost exactly a month later in September 2021 that my daughter started to make comments that she was bored. I would follow up with her preschool teacher, get a reassuring response, and yet nothing was actually done. October 2021 my daughter got RSV from school. She was briefly hospitalized and this was a first experience for her. My husband and I knew from parenting books and the growing knowledge about social and emotional awareness and trauma informed practices to talk openly about these experiences with her.

Unfortunately my daughter did not get this same support at school. It came to be a recurring theme that the support my husband and I were able to provide at home did not match the outdated information our daughter was getting at school. The teacher would openly complain about my daughter talking about her hospital experience, certain holidays like halloween that she loved, and eventually the biggest issue came when my daughter was pushed by another student and the school didn't alert us.

It finally came to a point that the school's only answer to our questions was to respond with formalized meetings that started as an SST or student support team meeting, that was a group of adults around a table collectively telling us to "wait and see". I learned from neurodiversity advocate books that this was a delay tactic documented as early as 1969 by a reading specialist named Alice Ansara. From October 2021 to spring of 2022 I started to learn about the history of whole language instruction in anticipation of listening to the Sold a Story podcast. I began to learn that the issues my husband and I were experiencing in public school were almost exactly the same in all 50 states of America in schools that had invested in an ineffective reading program by the name of "Balanced Literacy".

I started to read books by Rudolf Flesh, Jeanne Chall, and I started to follow the growing movement called Science of Reading online. I downloaded and purchased books on the history of reading instruction. I learned about the Reading Wars, Curriculum Wars, and the Math wars. I kept seeing a constant pattern of adults with egos trying to sell a product becoming the main problem between what worked and what did not.

It was finally in October the Sold a story podcast came out and validated the waves of emotion that I had been feeling. November 2022 after a failed IEP meeting or an individualized education plan meeting where we tried to get the school to formally recognize Dyslexia or a Specific Learning Disability for my daughter when my husband and I realized that it wasn't working. The school's firm position was that they had invested millions of dollars into Balanced Literacy and Round Robin Reading. They still used leveled reading books made by controversial whole languages and three cueing advocates. They did not care that my daughter was reading decodable books at home without an issue. They didn't care about my daughter sitting at a dinner table and crying when she couldn't get through a leveled reading book that had no scope or sequence to the words.

The last straw came when the school BCBA or a Board Certified Behavior Analyst, who was a proponent of behaviorism and ABA or applied behavior analysis had suggested that they touch my daughter by poking or physically moving her nap mat in order to wake her in Kindergarten. My husband and I firmly said no. The school's solution, since they didn't understand that a sign of unsupported dyslexia was exhaustion from learning, was that it was my responsibility as her mother to pick her up early from school at 12:00pm. I now understand this to be not supported by the federal education laws as an undocumented suspension.

What made matters worse was that it was exactly one day after this request that the paraprofessional in my daughter's kindergarten class pushed my daughter into a shelf in the classroom bathroom and it was misdocumented by the school nurse. The school dismissed the incident as an accident and never notified myself or my husband. It was only told to me in passing by the general education teacher during early pick up. I took my daughter to the pediatrician and they documented it was a hard enough push to bruise both of my daughter's knees. At this time we had a virtual therapist from all of the school issues. The therapist had recommended a change of classroom. The school refused. We attempted a request to change elementary schools entirely since there were two other schools in the district. I volunteered to drive my daughter daily to either one. The school refused.

We finally withdrew my daughter from brick and mortar public school in the first week of December of 2022.

Within three months of withdrawal, I took free Cox Campus Structured Literacy training, I took Microsoft Learn Dyslexia Training, and Nessy Learning Dyslexia training. My daughter's anxiety, and school refusal and boredom was gone. She was learning to read with a phonics based program and decodable texts. The more she practiced decoding and built up her phonemic and phonological awareness, her fluency with reading any text had improved. Today I am a wife of 9 years, a stay at home mom for 7 years, and a proud homeschool educator. I am deeply grateful and indebted to the two years I've spent learning from books, webinars, and online advocates that neurodiversity is a biological fact.

My daughter's reading issues were not because she wasn't good enough. They were not because she is lazy. They are not because she couldn't work hard enough at memorizing sight words. They are not because she couldn't memorize a repetitive text.

They absolutely were temporary issues due to the fact that the public school was sold a million dollar story. Balanced literacy does not work for neurodivergent brains. Whole language does not work for dyslexic or gifted brains. Three cuing or guessing at words in a leveled reading book does not teach any human brain to learn the neurobiological skill of reading.

<u>Reading is a skill that has to be taught.</u>

I actively advocate today on the fact that this is why parents are so important as a child's very first teacher. Parents through caregiving are the most fundamental form of mentorship and apprenticeship. We model a skill for our children. We perform that skill with our children. Then once our children develop the skill, the parent understands the process of gradual release of responsibility. We finally let our children perform the skill on their own with confidence and independence. This is wonderfully documented to apply to education, the classroom, any subject, but most importantly Structured Literacy by Dr. Anita Archer.

This is why I hope parents, professionals, educators, and advocates find this book, Astronomical Learning, to be a valuable part of helping to imagine a better future for not just one type of student, but all students that deserve a supportive, affordable or free, appropriate, inclusive, and diverse education.

Chapter 1: Introduction to Astronomical Learning

Astronomical learning refers to a comprehensive approach to education that aims to inspire and empower learners to reach new heights of understanding and achievement. This approach emphasizes the importance of family and community involvement of learning, structured literacy and math instruction, phonemic awareness, numeracy skills, explicit instruction, the gradual release of responsibility, and all while using a strength-based approach.

In the Astronomical Learning model, we celebrate the understanding of neurodiversity as a biological fact. Just as if we understand biodiversity in nature. Every human brain is fundamentally wired differently. I want to encourage people to reject the outdated notion of a one-size-fits-all education system and embrace the unique abilities, strengths, and challenges of every single individual.

What is the foundation of Astronomical Learning?

1. Family Literacy with Structured Literacy and Phonemic Awareness:

- Family literacy activities engage parents and caregivers in supporting children's literacy development from an early age. These activities include reading aloud, storytelling, writing, and language games.

- Structured literacy instruction provides explicit and systematic instruction in phonics, phonemic awareness, vocabulary, comprehension, and fluency. It offers a clear and consistent framework for teaching reading and writing skills.

- Phonemic awareness activities help children develop an understanding of the sounds of language and how they relate to written symbols. By explicitly teaching phonemic awareness skills, children learn to manipulate sounds and decode words more effectively.

2. Family Math with Structured Math and Number Sense:

- Family math activities involve parents and caregivers in promoting numeracy skills through everyday activities, games, and conversations about math concepts.

- Structured math instruction provides explicit and sequential teaching of mathematical concepts and procedures. It emphasizes problem-solving, reasoning, and mathematical fluency.

- Numbersense instruction focuses on developing a deep understanding of numerical relationships, operations, and mathematical reasoning. It helps students build flexibility and confidence in using numbers to solve problems and make connections across mathematical domains.

3. Explicit Instruction with Gradual Release of Responsibility:

- Explicit instruction involves clearly stating learning objectives, modeling skills and strategies, providing guided practice, and offering opportunities for independent application.

- The "gradual release of responsibility" model gradually shifts responsibility for learning from the teacher to the student. It begins with teacher modeling and guided practice and progresses to independent application by the student.

- This approach allows learners to build understanding and mastery of concepts and skills over time, with scaffolded support and opportunities for independent practice and application.

4. Strength-Based Approach:

- A strength-based approach focuses on identifying and leveraging learners' strengths, interests, and assets to support their learning and development.

- By recognizing and building on learners' strengths, educators and families can create positive learning experiences that foster motivation, confidence, and a sense of agency.

- This approach emphasizes the importance of valuing and affirming learners' diverse abilities and backgrounds, creating inclusive learning environments where all students can thrive.

In summary, astronomical learning is built on the foundation of family and community involvement, structured instruction in literacy and math, explicit teaching of phonemic awareness and Number Sense, the gradual release of responsibility, and a strength-based approach that recognizes and celebrates learners' unique strengths and capabilities. By integrating these components into educational practice, educators and families can empower learners to reach for the stars and achieve their full potential in learning and life.

Chapter 2: What is Family Literacy and Why is it important?

Family literacy refers to the ability of families to read, write, and communicate effectively together. It involves the development of literacy skills within the context of family relationships and everyday activities.

Family literacy encompasses various activities and practices that promote literacy skills among family members, including parents, children, and sometimes extended family members. These activities can include reading books together, telling stories, engaging in conversations, playing word games, writing notes or letters, and using literacy in daily routines such as cooking, shopping, and managing finances.

Family literacy programs often aim to enhance parents' literacy skills while also fostering a supportive environment for children's literacy development. These programs may provide resources, guidance, and support to help parents improve their reading and writing abilities, as well as strategies for incorporating literacy activities into family life.

The goal of family literacy is not only to improve individual literacy skills but also to strengthen family bonds, promote positive parent-child interactions, and create a home environment that values learning and education. By engaging in literacy activities together, families can build stronger relationships and empower each other to succeed academically and professionally.

<u>Family literacy skills play a crucial role in lifelong success for individuals and families.</u>

Astronomical Learning reasons why family literacy skills are important for lifelong success:

1. Foundation for Learning: Family literacy skills provide the foundation for lifelong learning and academic achievement. Children who are exposed to literacy-rich environments at home develop strong language skills, vocabulary, and comprehension abilities, which are essential for success in school and beyond.

2. Promotion of Literacy and Numeracy: Family literacy skills encompass not only reading and writing but also numeracy and mathematical abilities. By engaging in literacy and math activities with their families, children develop essential skills that are critical for navigating the complexities of modern life.

3. Improved Communication Skills: Family literacy activities promote effective communication skills, including listening, speaking, and writing. Children who engage in conversations, storytelling, and writing activities with their families develop the confidence and ability to express themselves clearly and effectively in various contexts.

4. Enhanced Critical Thinking and Problem-Solving: Family literacy activities stimulate critical thinking and problem-solving skills by encouraging children to analyze information, make connections, and draw conclusions. Through reading, writing, and math activities, children learn to think critically, evaluate evidence, and solve real-world problems.

5. Empowerment and Self-Advocacy: Family literacy empowers individuals to advocate for themselves and their communities. By developing literacy and numeracy skills, individuals gain the confidence and ability to access information, navigate systems, and participate fully in civic and social life.

6. Promotion of Health and Well-being: Literacy skills are essential for promoting health literacy and well-being. Individuals with strong literacy skills are better equipped to understand health information, make in-

formed decisions about their health, and access healthcare services effectively.

7. Increased Opportunities for Economic Success: Family literacy skills are closely linked to economic success and upward mobility. Individuals with higher levels of literacy and numeracy are more likely to secure stable employment, earn higher wages, and achieve financial independence.

8. Intergenerational Impact: Family literacy skills have a positive intergenerational impact, as parents and caregivers serve as role models and educators for their children. When parents prioritize literacy and numeracy in the home, they instill a love of learning and a commitment to education in future generations.

9. Community Engagement and Social Cohesion: Family literacy activities promote community engagement and social cohesion by bringing families together around shared learning experiences. By participating in literacy events, workshops, and programs, families build social connections, support networks, and a sense of belonging within their communities.

Overall, family literacy skills are fundamental to individual and collective success in all aspects of life. By fostering a culture of literacy and numeracy within families, communities, and society at large, we can create opportunities for everyone to thrive and fulfill their potential.

What does Family Literacy look like?

1. Reading Aloud: Start reading to your child from birth. Choose age-appropriate books with colorful pictures and simple texts. Reading aloud helps develop vocabulary, language skills, and a love for reading.

2. Rhymes and Songs: Sing nursery rhymes, songs, and fingerplays together. Rhymes help children develop phonemic awareness, rhythm, and language skills.

3. Storytelling:Encourage storytelling by asking open-ended questions and encouraging your child to describe events, characters, and settings. This promotes language development and creativity.

4. Book Exploration: Let your child explore books independently. Provide access to a variety of books and materials, and encourage them to flip through pages, point to pictures, and make observations.

5. Literacy-Rich Environment: Create a literacy-rich environment at home by labeling objects, displaying children's artwork and writing, and providing access to writing materials like crayons, markers, and paper.

Chapter 3: I keep hearing people say, "Just read to your kids, 5 minutes a day" or "They need to learn a love of reading first", is this true?

———

NO!

Reading has to be taught.

What some people misunderstand is the neurotype of Hyperlexia, or when a young child can read at levels far beyond those expected for their age. A child with hyperlexia might figure out how to decode or sound out words very quickly, but not understand or comprehend most of what they're reading. They still need structured literacy to better understand the connection between the grapheme, a phoneme, and a morpheme. If they only learn to break the alphabetic code by decoding or breaking down a word into the different sounds, they won't learn the meaning of that word. This hinders the ability to fully master the linguistic system of a language.

The human brain is wired for learning languages. The human brain is not wired to read without proper instruction.

Family literacy and the "love of reading" are related concepts but have distinct meanings:

1. Family Literacy:

- Family literacy refers to the practice of involving families in literacy-related activities, such as reading, writing, storytelling, and language games, to support children's literacy development.

- It encompasses a range of activities and interactions that promote literacy skills within the family context, including reading aloud to children, engaging in literacy-rich conversations, and providing opportunities for writing and creative expression.

- Family literacy programs often involve parents, caregivers, and other family members in supporting children's literacy development from an early age and throughout their educational journey.

2. Love of Reading:

- The "love of reading" refers to an individual's personal enjoyment, interest, and enthusiasm for reading books and other written materials.

- It is characterized by a positive emotional connection to reading, a desire to explore new ideas and perspectives through literature, and a sense of pleasure and fulfillment derived from the reading experience.

- The love of reading is often cultivated through exposure to diverse and engaging texts, positive reading experiences, and supportive reading environments that encourage curiosity, exploration, and personal expression.

While family literacy activities can play a significant role in fostering a love of reading, they are not synonymous.

Family literacy encompasses a broader range of literacy-related activities beyond reading alone, including writing, storytelling, and language play.

The love of reading, on the other hand, is a personal and emotional connection to reading that transcends specific literacy practices and encompasses a deep appreciation for the written word and its transformative power in shaping lives and perspectives.

You can absolutely learn to read without needing to love reading. I personally don't love to do chores, dishes, or laundry. Yet I know how to do these skills. I didn't have to love them before I learned to do them.

Chapter 4: What are the developmental stages of Phonemic Awareness?

——

Phonemic awareness is the ability to recognize and manipulate individual sounds, or phonemes, in spoken words.

It's a crucial skill that lays the foundation for reading and spelling. Here are the developmental stages of developing phonemic awareness in a child:

1. Awareness of Environmental Sounds (Ages 0-2): - Infants and toddlers begin by developing awareness of environmental sounds, such as birds chirping, cars honking, or water running.

- They listen to and discriminate between different sounds in their environment, laying the groundwork for auditory discrimination skills.

2. Recognizing Rhyme and Alliteration (Ages 2-3):

- Preschool-age children start to recognize and produce rhymes, such as words that end with the same sound (e.g., cat, hat).

- They enjoy playing with language through nursery rhymes, poems, and songs, which help them develop an ear for sounds.

- Children also begin to notice alliteration, or words that start with the same sound (e.g., big brown bear), further enhancing their phonemic awareness.

3. Segmenting and Blending Syllables (Ages 3-4):

- Children begin to break words into syllables, identifying the parts that make up longer words (e.g., um-brel-la).

- They also practice blending syllables together to form whole words, such as putting together "cat" and "dog" to say "catalog."

- Activities like clapping out syllables in words or playing with compound words help strengthen segmentation and blending skills.

4. Segmenting and Blending Phonemes (Ages 4-5):

- Children progress to segmenting and blending individual phonemes, the smallest units of sound in language.

- They learn to isolate and identify the initial, medial, and final sounds in words

(e.g., cat → /k/ /a/ /t/).

- Activities like sound matching games, word manipulation (e.g., changing the beginning sound of a word), and phoneme substitution exercises help develop phonemic awareness skills.

5. Manipulating Phonemes (Ages 5 and Beyond):

- As children's phonemic awareness continues to develop, they gain the ability to manipulate phonemes within words.

- They can add, delete, or substitute phonemes to create new words

(e.g., changing "cat" to "hat" by substituting the initial sound).

- Phonemic awareness activities become more advanced, including phoneme segmentation and blending tasks, phoneme deletion and substitution tasks, and phoneme categorization exercises.

6. Application to Reading and Spelling (Ages 6 and Beyond):

- Phonemic awareness forms the basis for learning to read and spell. Children use their understanding of phonemes to decode unfamiliar words and spell words phonetically.

- They develop strategies for sounding out words, recognizing word patterns, and using context clues to understand meaning.

- Continued practice and exposure to print-rich environments support the integration of phonemic awareness skills into reading and spelling tasks.

By understanding the developmental stages of phonemic awareness, parents and educators can provide appropriate support and activities to help children develop this critical foundational skill for literacy.

Chapter 5: What are the developmental stages of Reading?

⸻

I highly recommend reading the books and work of Jeanne Chall to understand the developmental stages of reading. Her work provides valuable insights into the stages of reading development, which can be aligned with structured literacy principles.

1. Pre-Reading Stage (Birth to Kindergarten): - Focus: Developing foundational skills for literacy acquisition.

- Activities: Exposure to spoken language, rhymes, songs, and stories; developing phonological awareness; exploring print concepts; building vocabulary through oral language experiences.

2. Initial Reading or Decoding Stage (Kindergarten to Grade 1): - Focus: Learning letter-sound correspondences and decoding skills.

- Activities: Letter-sound recognition; phonemic awareness activities; decoding simple, decodable texts; sight word recognition; developing fluency through repeated reading.

3. Confirmation, Fluency, and Unbound Reading Stage (Grades 2-3): - Focus: Developing fluency, automaticity, and comprehension.

- Activities: Continued phonics instruction with more complex phonics patterns; expanding vocabulary; reading connected text with expression and fluency; developing comprehension strategies; exploring different genres of literature.

4. Reading to Learn the New (Grades 4-8):

- Focus: Transitioning from learning to read to reading to learn.

- Activities: Reading increasingly complex texts across content areas; deepening comprehension skills through inferential and critical thinking; analyzing text structure and author's purpose; building academic vocabulary; writing to express understanding.

5. Multiple Viewpoints (Grades 9-12 and Beyond):

- Focus: Analyzing texts critically and synthesizing information from multiple sources.

- Activities: Engaging with diverse texts representing various perspectives; evaluating arguments and evidence; synthesizing information from multiple sources; developing advanced reading and writing skills for academic and professional contexts.

When educational instruction is aligned with Chall's stages, structured literacy instruction emphasizes systematic, explicit instruction in phonemic awareness, phonics, vocabulary, fluency, and comprehension at each developmental level.

Instruction is scaffolded to support students' progression through increasingly complex text and literacy tasks.

Structured literacy approaches incorporate evidence-based practices such as multisensory instruction, direct and explicit teaching of phonics rules and patterns, systematic decoding instruction, vocabulary development, and comprehension strategies. By addressing the neurodiverse needs of learners at each stage of development, structured literacy instruction promotes strong foundational skills and empowers students to become proficient readers and critical thinkers across grade levels.

Chapter 6: How can I build a Structured Literacy Curriculum?

———

Building a structured literacy curriculum for kindergarten through fifth-grade students at various stages of learning to read requires careful planning and alignment with developmental milestones and literacy benchmarks.

1. Assessment and Differentiation:

- Begin by assessing each student's current literacy skills, including phonemic awareness, phonics knowledge, vocabulary, fluency, and comprehension abilities.

- Use diagnostic assessments to identify areas of strength and areas needing improvement for each student.

- Differentiate instruction based on students' individual needs and learning styles.

2. Scope and Sequence:

- Develop a scope and sequence that outlines the progression of skills and concepts to be taught from kindergarten through fifth grade.

- Organize the curriculum into sequential units or modules, starting with foundational skills and gradually increasing in complexity.

3. Foundational Skills:

- Focus on building foundational skills such as phonemic awareness, letter-sound correspondence, phonics, decoding, encoding, and sight word recognition.

- Incorporate multisensory activities, games, songs, and hands-on manipulatives to engage young learners and reinforce key concepts.

4. Phonological and Phonemic Awareness:

- Include activities to develop phonological and phonemic awareness skills, such as identifying and manipulating individual sounds, blending and segmenting sounds in words, and recognizing rhyme and alliteration.

5. Phonics and Word Recognition:

- Teach phonics patterns, spelling rules, and word families systematically, using explicit instruction, modeling, and guided practice.

- Provide opportunities for students to apply phonics skills in reading and writing contexts, including decodable texts, word sorts, and word building activities.

6. Vocabulary Development:

- Introduce new vocabulary words and concepts through rich literature, informational texts, and content-based instruction.

- Teach strategies for determining the meaning of unknown words through context clues, word analysis, and morphological awareness.

7. Fluency Practice:

- Offer opportunities for repeated reading of texts at students' instructional levels to develop fluency, expression, and prosody.

- Provide model readings, choral reading, echo reading, reader's theater, and other fluency-building activities.

8. Comprehension Strategies:

- Teach a variety of comprehension strategies, such as predicting, summarizing, visualizing, questioning, making connections, and monitoring comprehension.

- Model think-alouds and scaffolded instruction to help students develop metacognitive awareness and strategic reading skills.

9. Integration and Application:

- Integrate literacy instruction across content areas, including science, social studies, and math, to reinforce and extend learning.

- Provide opportunities for students to apply reading and writing skills in authentic, meaningful contexts, such as projects, presentations, and discussions.

10. Assessment and Progress Monitoring:

- Implement ongoing formative assessments to monitor student progress and adjust instruction as needed.

- Use benchmark assessments and standardized tests to evaluate overall literacy growth and identify areas for targeted intervention.

By following these guidelines and incorporating evidence-based practices, you can design a comprehensive structured literacy curriculum that supports the diverse needs of kindergarten through fifth-grade students as they develop essential reading skills.

Additionally, leveraging online platforms can provide flexibility, accessibility, and interactive learning experiences for students in both individual and group settings.

Chapter 7: What is the best type of assessment?

———

I have a personal preference for an errorless assessment for determining a tutoring client's mastery of the 44 phonemes before instruction starts that can be designed to identify their existing knowledge and areas that require focus.

I like to think of an errorless assessment as a friendly check-in to see where your student or child is excelling and where they might need a little extra support.

It's done in a positive and supportive way, without focusing too much on mistakes. Instead, it helps us see what your child is already great at and what we can work on together to help them grow even more.

The key thing about errorless assessment is that it's not about judging your child or putting pressure on them to get everything right. It's about creating a safe and supportive environment where they can show us what they know and where they might need some help. This way, we can tailor our teaching approach to best meet their needs and help them succeed.

By understanding how your child is doing through errorless assessment, we can celebrate their successes and provide targeted support where it's needed. It's all about helping your child reach their full potential and making sure they feel confident and supported along the way.

———

WHAT DOES AN ASTRONOMICAL Learning Literacy Assessment look like?

Materials Needed:

ASTRONOMICAL LEARNING

1. Phoneme assessment sheet or digital platform for recording responses.

2. Phoneme cards or word lists representing each phoneme.

Procedure:

1. Introduction (5 minutes):

- Explain the purpose of the assessment: to identify the client's current understanding of phonemes.

- Provide instructions on how to complete the assessment: listen to the phoneme or word and identify the corresponding phoneme sound.

2. Phoneme Identification Task (20 minutes):

- Present each phoneme individually, either through auditory presentation or visual representation.

- Ask the client to identify the phoneme sound they hear.

- Record their responses on the assessment sheet or digital platform.

3. Word List Identification Task (20 minutes):

- Present a series of words, each containing one of the 44 phonemes.

- Ask the client to identify the phoneme sound in each word.

- Record their responses, noting any patterns of errors or consistent difficulties.

4. Assessment Review and Discussion (10 minutes):

- Review the client's responses and identify areas of strength and areas needing improvement. - Discuss any patterns of errors or specific phonemes that were challenging for the client.

- Provide feedback and encouragement, emphasizing the importance of phonemic awareness in reading and spelling.

Scoring:

- Evaluate the client's responses based on accuracy in identifying the phoneme sounds.

- Note any phonemes that were consistently missed or misunderstood.

- Determine the overall level of mastery of the 44 phonemes based on the client's performance.

Considerations:

- Ensure a supportive and encouraging atmosphere during the assessment to alleviate any anxiety or pressure.

- Use a variety of words and phonemes to capture the client's full range of knowledge and skills.- Provide clear instructions and examples to clarify the task and expectations.

By conducting an errorless assessment before instruction starts, you can gain valuable insights into the client's baseline phonemic awareness skills and tailor the tutoring program to address their specific needs and areas for growth. When you are emphasizing the positive and supportive nature of errorless assessment and its role in personalized learning, parents can better understand its importance in their child's educational experience.

Chapter 8: How do I know if my child, student, or client lacks developmental reading skills?

Without phonemic awareness, students may struggle to recognize and manipulate individual sounds in words, leading to difficulties in decoding and encoding written language.

- They may have trouble breaking words into their component sounds, blending sounds together to form words, and segmenting words into their individual sounds.

- Without these phonemic awareness skills, students may struggle with reading fluency and comprehension, as they may have difficulty sounding out words and understanding the relationships between letters and sounds.

- Students may experience frustration and disengagement with reading and writing tasks, which can impact their overall academic performance and self-esteem.

How do I know if I myself or a parent or a community member is an adult and lacks developmental reading skills?

A lack of phonemic awareness in adults can manifest in various ways and may impact different aspects of their language and literacy skills.

Here are some signs and examples of what it might look like in adults:

1. Difficulty with Reading and Spelling:

- Adults lacking phonemic awareness may struggle with decoding written words, especially unfamiliar or multisyllabic words.

- They may have difficulty recognizing and applying phonics rules, which can lead to errors in spelling and pronunciation.

2. Limited Vocabulary Development:

- Individuals lacking phonemic awareness may have a limited vocabulary and struggle to learn new words, particularly those with complex phonetic structures.

- They may rely heavily on context clues or memorization rather than decoding words phonetically.

3. Poor Reading Fluency and Comprehension:

- Adults with a lack of phonemic awareness may read slowly and laboriously, as they struggle to segment and blend sounds to form words.

- They may have difficulty understanding the meaning of written texts, as decoding challenges impede their ability to comprehend sentences and passages effectively.

4. Difficulty with Oral Language Skills:

- Individuals lacking phonemic awareness may have difficulty discriminating between similar-sounding words or distinguishing subtle phonetic differences in spoken language.

- They may struggle with articulation and pronunciation, leading to challenges in oral communication and language expression.

5. Limited Phonological Processing Abilities:

- Adults lacking phonemic awareness may have difficulty manipulating sounds within words, such as blending, segmenting, or deleting phonemes.

- They may find it challenging to engage in phonological awareness tasks, such as rhyming, syllable counting, or identifying initial, medial, and final sounds in words.

6. Struggles with Spelling and Writing:

- Individuals with a lack of phonemic awareness may struggle with spelling accuracy and consistency, as they have difficulty mapping sounds to letters and vice versa.

- They may rely on visual memorization or guesswork when spelling words, leading to frequent spelling errors and inconsistencies in written communication.

Overall, a lack of phonemic awareness in adults can significantly impact their ability to effectively decode, encode, and comprehend written language. However, it's important to note that phonemic awareness is a skill that can be developed and improved through targeted instruction, phonics instruction, and literacy interventions.

Community implemented adult literacy programs, speech-language therapy, and phonological awareness training can help individuals enhance their phonemic awareness skills and improve their overall literacy abilities.

Chapter 9 : Is everyone who has reading difficulties considered Dyslexic?

No!

There is a fundamental difference between someone who has not been taught to read and a Dyslexic person. Someone who has not been effectively taught to read means they have not received instruction or exposure to reading skills and literacy practices. This could be due to various factors such as lack of access to education, limited resources, cultural barriers, or limited opportunities for learning to read.

In this case, the individual's difficulty with reading is primarily a result of not having been taught the necessary skills and strategies for reading proficiency. Once provided with appropriate instruction and support, individuals who have not been taught to read can typically learn to read and improve their literacy skills with time and practice.

Dyslexia, on the other hand, is a specific learning disability that is a neurotype and affects reading and language processing skills. It is characterized by difficulties with accurate and fluent word recognition, spelling, and decoding abilities. It is a language based neurotype and is not due to visual issues.

Individuals with dyslexia may experience challenges in phonological processing, which involves recognizing and manipulating the sounds of language. They may struggle with letter-sound correspondence, decoding unfamiliar words, and recognizing high frequency words.

Dyslexia is neurobiological in nature and is believed to result from differences in the way the brain processes language, particularly in the areas responsible for reading and phonological processing.

Unlike individuals who have not been taught to read, individuals with dyslexia may receive instruction in reading but still encounter persistent difficulties despite adequate teaching and support. Dyslexic students benefit from Structured Literacy and is a lifelong different brain wiring. It can not be "corrected" or "cured". It also has its own social and emotional challenges depending on the individual and their experiences.

Chapter 10: Can you ever be too old to learn to read?

N O!

It's imperative to explain the importance of phonemic awareness to an older student who can help them understand how it can enhance their reading and spelling skills, at any age.

<u>Here are some key points to consider:</u>

1. Understanding Speech Sounds: Phonemic awareness involves the ability to hear, identify, and manipulate individual sounds, or phonemes, in spoken words. Even for older students, this skill is crucial because it helps them break down words into their constituent sounds, which is essential for accurate reading and spelling.

2. Reading Fluency: Older students who struggle with reading may find that improving their phonemic awareness can enhance their reading fluency. By being able to identify and manipulate individual sounds in words, they can decode unfamiliar words more easily and read with greater speed and accuracy.

3. Spelling Skills: Phonemic awareness also plays a significant role in spelling. When students can segment words into phonemes and manipulate those sounds, they are better equipped to spell words accurately. Understanding the sound-letter correspondence helps them make informed choices when spelling words.

4. Vocabulary Development: By developing phonemic awareness, older students can also expand their vocabulary. When they can hear and ma-

nipulate sounds in words, they are better able to discern word meanings and make connections between words with similar sounds or spelling patterns.

5. Building Confidence: Improving phonemic awareness can boost a student's confidence in their reading and spelling abilities. As they gain proficiency in recognizing and manipulating sounds, they become more confident in their skills and are more likely to approach reading and spelling tasks with greater assurance.

6. Closing Achievement Gaps: For older students who may have struggled with reading and spelling for years, developing phonemic awareness can help close achievement gaps. By addressing foundational skills that may have been overlooked or underdeveloped, students can make significant strides in their literacy skills.

7. Lifelong Learning: Finally, phonemic awareness is not just important for reading and spelling in school but also for lifelong learning. Strong phonemic awareness skills can benefit students in their academic pursuits and beyond, enabling them to effectively comprehend and communicate through written language in various contexts.

Overall, while older students may initially feel that phonemic awareness is a skill more suited for younger children, they can still benefit greatly from its development. By recognizing the importance of phonemic awareness and engaging in targeted practice, older students can improve their reading, spelling, and overall literacy skills, setting a strong foundation for future academic and personal success.

Chapter 11: How do I know if my child's school has a Structured Literacy Curriculum?

#1. Find out what kind of instruction your child is getting or has gotten in school.

#2. Sight word list memorization, Levelled Reader books labeled by Alphabet letters, or the teacher telling a student to "Look at the picture" or "Use context clues" instead of helping a student break down the word into the individual sounds are a bright red flag.

How do I know if my student is stuck at the Emergent Reader Stage?

- Without explicit and direct instruction in the 44 phonemes of the English language, students may struggle to decode words accurately and fluently.

- Phonemic awareness, the ability to hear, identify, and manipulate individual sounds in words, is essential for successful decoding.

Without phonemic awareness instruction, students may have difficulty segmenting and blending sounds to read and spell words.

- Some students may rely heavily on guessing or memorizing whole words rather than applying phonics principles to decode unfamiliar words.

- Lack of explicit instruction in phonics can lead to gaps in students' understanding of letter-sound relationships and phonics rules, hindering their ability to decode and encode words independently.

What can I do if my child's school doesn't have a Structured Literacy Cur-

riculum?

#1. Advocate for Explicit Phonics Instruction: Encourage schools to provide systematic and explicit phonics instruction as part of their literacy curriculum.

2. Supplement with Phonics Activities at Home: Engage your child in phonics-based activities, such as word-building games, phonemic awareness exercises, and decoding practice with decodable texts.

3. Provide Access to Phonics Resources: Invest in phonics workbooks, flashcards, and online resources that reinforce letter-sound correspondences and phonics rules.

4. Read Aloud and Discuss Texts: Continue reading aloud to your child and engage in discussions about the text. Encourage them to ask questions and make predictions based on context.

5. Monitor Progress and Seek Support if Needed: Keep an eye on your child's reading progress and reach out to teachers or literacy specialists if you have concerns about their development or if they seem to be struggling with decoding skills.

By understanding the limitations of whole language and balanced literacy approaches, parents

Chapter 12: What is Family Math and Why is it important?

F amily math refers to the practice of engaging in mathematical activities and discussions as a family to promote mathematical understanding, problem-solving skills, and a positive attitude towards math.

Family math involves parents and children working together on mathematical activities, games, and real-life math situations in an interactive and enjoyable manner. It encourages parents to incorporate math into everyday activities and conversations, such as cooking, budgeting, shopping, and playing games.

<u>Family math ability plays a significant role in lifelong success for individuals and families.</u>

Here are several reasons why family math ability is important for lifelong success:

1. Foundation for Academic Achievement: Family math ability provides a strong foundation for academic achievement and success in school. Children who engage in math activities with their families develop essential numeracy skills, critical thinking abilities, and problem-solving strategies that are essential for learning and mastering mathematical concepts.

2. Development of Numeracy Skills: Numeracy skills are crucial for navigating everyday tasks, making informed decisions, and solving real-life problems. By engaging in math activities at home, children develop numeracy skills such as counting, measuring, estimating, and comparing quantities, which are essential for success in various aspects of life.

3. Enhanced Critical Thinking and Problem-Solving: Family math activities stimulate critical thinking and problem-solving skills by encouraging children to analyze situations, apply mathematical principles, and explore different solutions. By engaging in mathematical reasoning and problem-solving, children develop the confidence and ability to tackle challenges in academic, professional, and personal contexts.

4. Promotion of Logical Reasoning and Spatial Skills: Family math activities promote logical reasoning and spatial skills by encouraging children to think logically, visualize spatial relationships, and manipulate objects in their environment. These skills are valuable for understanding abstract mathematical concepts, as well as for success in fields such as science, technology, engineering, and mathematics (STEM).

5. Preparation for Financial Literacy: Family math ability prepares children for financial literacy and responsible money management. By engaging in activities such as budgeting, saving, and comparing prices, children learn valuable financial skills that are essential for making informed financial decisions and planning for the future.

6. Empowerment and Self-Efficacy: Family math activities empower children to see themselves as capable and confident problem solvers. By experiencing success and mastery in math-related tasks with their families, children develop a positive attitude towards math and a belief in their ability to succeed in challenging academic and professional pursuits.

7. Promotion of Lifelong Learning: Family math ability fosters a culture of lifelong learning within families, where curiosity, exploration, and discovery are valued. By engaging in math-related activities together, families promote a love of learning and a sense of curiosity that extends beyond the classroom and into all aspects of life.

8. Interdisciplinary Connections: Math is interconnected with other dis-

ciplines, including science, technology, engineering, art, and music. Family math activities provide opportunities for children to explore these interdisciplinary connections, fostering creativity, innovation, and interdisciplinary thinking skills that are essential for success in a rapidly changing world.

Overall, family math ability is essential for fostering academic achievement, promoting critical thinking and problem-solving skills, preparing children for financial literacy, and fostering a lifelong love of learning. By engaging in math-related activities together, families can empower children to succeed academically, professionally, and personally, and to become confident, capable, and competent mathematicians and problem solvers.

Chapter 13: What does Family Math look like?

1. Counting Games: Incorporate counting into everyday activities, such as counting toys, steps, or snacks. Use counting songs and rhymes to make learning fun.

2. Number Recognition: Point out numbers in the environment, such as on clocks, calendars, and signs. Play games that involve matching, sorting, and recognizing numbers.

3. Exploration of Shapes and Patterns: Encourage exploration of shapes and patterns through play and everyday objects. Look for shapes in the environment and create patterns using toys, blocks, or household items.

4. Measurement and Comparison: Introduce concepts of measurement and comparison through hands-on activities. Let your child measure ingredients while cooking or compare the sizes of objects during play.

5. Problem-Solving Activities: Engage in problem-solving activities that involve puzzles, building blocks, and simple math games. Encourage your child to think critically and find solutions to challenges.

What are the developmental stages of math abilities?

It's usually called Number Sense, or numerical understanding, develops gradually as children grow and interact with their environment.

Here's a general overview of the developmental stages of number sense in children:

1. Early Numeracy (Ages 0-3): - Infants begin to develop an awareness of quantity through sensory experiences, such as seeing and touching ob-

jects.

- They start to recognize basic numerical concepts, like "more" and "less," through simple comparisons.

- Early numeracy skills emerge through daily routines, such as counting fingers or recognizing familiar objects.

2. Counting and Number Recognition (Ages 3-5):

- Preschool-age children start to understand the concept of counting and begin to recite numbers in order.

- They may recognize and identify numerals and associate them with quantities. - Children engage in informal counting activities, such as counting objects, steps, or claps, to develop basic counting skills.

- They start to understand one-to-one correspondence, associating each object with one number as they count.

3. Understanding Quantity and Relationships (Ages 5-7):

- Children develop a deeper understanding of quantity, recognizing that numbers represent specific quantities of objects.

- They begin to grasp basic arithmetic concepts, such as addition and subtraction, through hands-on experiences and manipulatives.

- Children explore relationships between numbers, such as understanding that 6 is greater than 4 and less than 8.

- They may use visual representations, like ten frames or number lines, to model and solve simple mathematical problems.

4. Numerical Operations and Problem-Solving (Ages 7-10):

- Children refine their understanding of addition, subtraction, multiplication, and division, applying strategies to solve mathematical problems.

- They develop fluency in basic arithmetic operations and learn to use mental math strategies to solve problems efficiently.

- Children begin to understand the properties of numbers, such as commutativity and associativity, and apply them in problem-solving situations.

- They use concrete and abstract models to represent mathematical concepts and solve multi-step problems.

5. Abstract Reasoning and Mathematical Thinking (Ages 10 and Beyond):

- As children progress through elementary and middle school, they develop more abstract reasoning skills and apply them to advanced mathematical concepts.

- They explore concepts like fractions, decimals, percentages, ratios, and algebraic equations.

- Children develop problem-solving skills, logical reasoning, and the ability to communicate mathematical ideas effectively.

- They apply mathematical concepts and skills to real-world situations, making connections between mathematics and other disciplines.

Throughout these developmental stages, children build on their previous experiences and knowledge to deepen their understanding of numbers and mathematical concepts. Parents, caregivers, and educators play a crucial role in nurturing children's number sense by providing rich mathematical experiences and opportunities for exploration and discovery.

Chapter 14: How do I know if my child or student or client lacks Number Sense?

Without number sense, students may struggle to understand basic numerical concepts, such as counting, comparing quantities, and performing simple arithmetic operations.

- They may have difficulty recognizing and understanding number symbols and their relationships, making it challenging to solve mathematical problems and understand mathematical concepts.

- Students may struggle with basic math skills, such as addition, subtraction, multiplication, and division, which are essential for success in later grades and everyday life.

- Without a strong foundation in number sense, students may develop math anxiety and a negative attitude towards mathematics, affecting their confidence and motivation to learn.

Is there a Specific Learning Disability that is connected to Math?

YES!

Dyscalculia is characterized by persistent difficulties in math despite receiving instruction and support. It is not simply a result of lack of effort or inadequate teaching.

Dyscalculia can vary in severity from person to person and may coexist with other learning disabilities, such as dyslexia or ADHD. Early identification and appropriate intervention can help individuals with dyscalculia develop strategies to compensate for their difficulties and improve their mathematical abilities.

It's important to note that dyscalculia is a neurological condition, or a neurotype, and not a reflection of a person's intelligence or effort. With appropriate support and accommodations, individuals with dyscalculia can succeed academically and develop strategies to navigate mathematical challenges in their daily lives.

Chapter 15: What does a lack of Number Sense look like in adults?

A lack of number sense in adults can manifest in various ways and may impact different aspects of their daily lives.

Here are some signs and examples of what a lack of number sense might look like in adults:

1. Difficulty with Basic Math Skills:

- Adults with a lack of number sense may struggle with basic arithmetic operations such as addition, subtraction, multiplication, and division.

- They may have difficulty mentally calculating simple sums or determining appropriate quantities when cooking, shopping, or budgeting.

2. Mismanagement of Finances:

- Individuals lacking number sense may struggle with financial management tasks such as budgeting, calculating interest rates, understanding loan terms, and managing debt.

- They may have difficulty comprehending financial statements, making informed financial decisions, and planning for the future.

3. Difficulty Estimating and Comparing Quantities:

- Adults with a lack of number sense may have difficulty estimating quantities, distances, or measurements in real-world contexts.

- They may struggle to compare prices, sizes, or amounts effectively when making purchasing decisions or evaluating options.

4. Limited Problem-Solving Abilities:

- Individuals lacking number sense may find it challenging to solve mathematical problems or analyze numerical data in various contexts.

- They may struggle with tasks that require logical reasoning, critical thinking, and quantitative analysis.

5. Difficulty Understanding Numerical Information:

- Adults with a lack of number sense may have difficulty interpreting numerical information presented in graphs, charts, tables, or reports.

- They may struggle to extract relevant information, draw conclusions, or make informed decisions based on numerical data.

6. Limited Numerical Literacy:

- Individuals lacking number sense may have limited numerical literacy, which can impact their ability to engage with quantitative information in everyday life, work, and social contexts.

- They may feel intimidated by numbers and avoid situations that require numerical reasoning or computation.

Overall, a lack of number sense in adults can impede their ability to navigate and succeed in a world that relies heavily on numerical information and mathematical reasoning. However, it's important to note that number sense is a skill that can be developed and improved with practice, education, and support. Adult education programs, financial literacy courses, and numeracy interventions can help individuals enhance their number sense and build confidence in their mathematical abilities.

Chapter 16: What does a Structured Math Curriculum look like?

A structured math curriculum in a school should be comprehensive, sequential, and aligned with educational standards to ensure that students receive a well-rounded mathematics education.

Here's a general overview of what parents can look for in a structured math curriculum:

1. Scope and Sequence: The curriculum should outline the scope, content coverage, and sequence , order of topics, of mathematical concepts and skills to be taught at each grade level. It should provide a clear roadmap for progression from basic to more complex mathematical ideas.

2. Alignment with Standards: The curriculum should align with state or national mathematics standards, such as the Common Core State Standards in the United States, which define the mathematical knowledge and skills that students should acquire at each grade level.

3. Conceptual Understanding: A strong math curriculum emphasizes conceptual understanding over memorization of procedures. It should include opportunities for students to explore mathematical concepts, make connections between mathematical ideas, and develop deep understanding through hands-on activities, problem-solving tasks, and real-world applications.

4. Problem-Solving and Reasoning: The curriculum should incorporate opportunities for students to engage in problem-solving activities and develop critical thinking and reasoning skills. Students should be encouraged to apply mathematical strategies, analyze problems from mul-

tiple perspectives, and communicate their mathematical thinking effectively.

5. Differentiated Instruction: A good math curriculum recognizes that students have diverse learning needs and provides differentiated instruction to support students at various levels of readiness and ability. It should include strategies for adapting instruction, providing additional support for struggling students, and offering enrichment opportunities for advanced learners.

6. Assessment and Feedback: The curriculum should include regular assessments, both formative and summative, to monitor students' progress, identify areas of strength and weakness, and inform instructional decisions. Teachers should provide timely and constructive feedback to students to help them reflect on their learning and set goals for improvement.

7. Technology Integration: A modern math curriculum may incorporate technology tools and resources to enhance instruction, facilitate interactive learning experiences, and provide opportunities for personalized learning. This could include educational software, interactive whiteboards, online tutorials, and digital manipulatives.

8. Parental Involvement and Communication: The school should involve parents in their children's mathematical learning by providing resources, information, and opportunities for involvement. Clear communication between teachers and parents about the math curriculum, instructional goals, and student progress is essential for fostering a supportive learning environment.

Chapter 17: What does an Astronomical Learning Structured Math Assessment look like?

An errorless assessment for structured math, particularly focusing on number sense, aims to identify a student's understanding of fundamental mathematical concepts without inducing frustration or anxiety associated with making mistakes. Here's an example of an errorless assessment for number sense:

Assessment: Number Sense Activity

Objective: To assess the student's understanding of basic number concepts, including counting, number recognition, and basic arithmetic operations.

Materials Needed:

-Number cards (1-10)

-Counters or manipulatives

-Blank paper

-Pencil or marker

Procedure of Number Recognition:

Show the student a set of number cards (1-10) one at a time.

Ask the student to identify each number verbally or point to the corresponding number card.

Record the student's responses on a separate sheet of paper.

ASTRONOMICAL LEARNING

Counting:

Provide the student with a set of counters or manipulatives.

Ask the student to count out a specific number of objects (e.g., "Show me three counters").

Gradually increase the complexity by asking the student to count forward or backward from a given number.

Procedure of Basic Arithmetic Operations:

Present simple addition and subtraction problems using manipulatives or visual aids.

Provide concrete examples, such as counting objects or using pictures to represent quantities.

Allow the student to demonstrate their understanding of addition (e.g., combining sets of objects) and subtraction (e.g., taking away objects).

Number Sequencing:

Give the student a sequence of numbers with missing elements.

Ask the student to fill in the missing numbers in the sequence.

Start with simple sequences and gradually increase the difficulty based on the student's ability.

Comparing Quantities:

Present the student with pairs of objects or groups of objects.

Ask the student to determine which group has more, fewer, or the same number of objects.

Use visual aids or manipulatives to support the comparison process.

Scoring and Interpretation:

-Assess the student's responses based on accuracy and understanding of number concepts.

Note any patterns of errors or areas of difficulty observed during the assessment.

-Provide positive reinforcement and encouragement throughout the assessment to create a supportive learning environment.

-Use the results of the assessment to inform instructional planning and tailor interventions to address areas of need.

By conducting an errorless assessment focused on number sense, educators can gain valuable insights into a student's mathematical understanding and tailor instruction to support their ongoing learning and development in mathematics.

Chapter 18: How can I combine both Family Literacy and Math in my home?

Incorporating Literacy and Math Skills:

1. Integrated Activities: Look for opportunities to integrate literacy and math skills into everyday routines and activities. For example, involve your child in cooking activities where they can follow recipes (literacy) and measure ingredients (math).

2. Interactive Play: Engage in interactive play that incorporates both literacy and math elements. Play games like "I Spy" to practice observation skills, vocabulary, and counting.

3. Outdoor Exploration: Take advantage of outdoor experiences to explore nature, numbers, and letters. Count leaves, identify shapes in clouds, and collect objects to sort and categorize.

4. Art and Creativity: Encourage artistic expression through drawing, painting, and storytelling. Children can create their own books, write stories, and illustrate them, promoting literacy and creativity.

5. Modeling and Participation: Model positive attitudes towards literacy and math by demonstrating enthusiasm for reading, writing, and problem-solving. Involve your child in family activities that require literacy and math skills, such as making grocery lists or planning outings.

By incorporating literacy and math skills into everyday activities and fostering a supportive learning environment at home, parents and caregivers can help children develop strong foundations in both areas and set them on the path to academic success.

Chapter 19: What is Explicit Instruction with Gradual Release of Responsibility?

Imagine you're learning how to ride a bike with your parents or teacher.

The "I do, we do, you do" gradual release of responsibility is like a fun way to learn step by step.

1. I do: First, your parent or teacher shows you how to ride the bike. They demonstrate by riding the bike themselves and explain how to balance and pedal. You watch them carefully to see how it's done.

2. We do: Next, it's time for both of you to ride together. Your parent or teacher holds onto the back of the bike while you sit on it. They help you balance and pedal, but you're also trying it out on your own. You're learning together as a team.

3. You do: Now comes the exciting part! Your parent or teacher lets go of the bike, and it's all up to you to ride.

They're there to cheer you on and support you if you need help, but you're doing most of the riding all by yourself.

You're taking charge and showing what you've learned!

So, the gradual release of responsibility is like learning to ride a bike with help at first, then practicing together, and finally, riding confidently all on your own. It's a super cool way to learn new things and become a pro!

What does it look like in education?

Explicit instruction and the gradual release of responsibility are effective instructional approaches that can be incorporated into family literacy and family math activities to support learning and skill development.

In family literacy and family math, explicit instruction involves clearly and directly teaching specific skills, strategies, and concepts to family members in a structured and systematic manner. Here's how to incorporate explicit instruction:

1. Identify Learning Objectives: Clearly define the learning objectives or goals of the literacy or math activity. What specific skills or concepts do you want family members to learn or practice?

2. Modeling: Demonstrate the targeted skill or strategy to family members through modeling. This could involve reading aloud with expression, demonstrating how to solve a math problem step by step, or explaining a literacy or math concept using examples.

3. Guided Practice: Provide opportunities for family members to practice the skill or strategy with guidance and support. Offer prompts, cues, and feedback as needed to scaffold their learning and help them apply the skill independently.

4. Feedback and Reinforcement: Offer constructive feedback and positive reinforcement to family members as they practice the skill or strategy. Encourage persistence and effort, and acknowledge their progress and achievements.

5. Explicit Instructional Materials: Use instructional materials such as books, worksheets, manipulatives, and online resources that are explicitly designed to support family literacy and math learning. Choose materials that are engaging, accessible, and relevant to family members' interests and experiences.

Gradual Release of Responsibility:

The gradual release of responsibility is a framework that involves gradually shifting the responsibility for learning from the teacher or parent to the learner. Here's how to incorporate the gradual release of responsibility into family literacy and family math activities:

1. Modeling (I do): Begin by modeling the literacy or math activity for family members, demonstrating how to perform the task or solve the problem. Think aloud and explain the thought process behind your actions to make the thinking visible.

2. Guided Practice (We do): Engage family members in collaborative practice activities where you work together to complete the literacy or math task. Provide guidance, support, and feedback as needed, and encourage active participation and shared problem-solving.

3. Independent Practice (You do): Gradually transition family members to independent practice, where they have the opportunity to apply the skills and strategies they've learned on their own. Encourage autonomy, self-monitoring, and reflection as they engage in literacy and math activities independently.

4. Reflection and Review: Foster opportunities for family members to reflect on their learning experiences and review their progress. Encourage open dialogue, ask probing questions, and facilitate discussions that promote metacognition and deeper understanding.

By incorporating explicit instruction and the gradual release of responsibility into family literacy and family math activities, you can create a supportive and empowering learning environment where family members can develop essential literacy and math skills while building strong bonds and shared experiences.

Chapter 20: How do we know this actually works?

———

Recent neuroscience research, including studies on mirror neurons, provides insights into how explicit instruction can be supported by understanding how the brain learns and processes information. Here's how neuroscience and mirror neurons can help explain the concept of explicit instruction:

1. Neuroplasticity and Learning: Neuroscience has revealed that the brain is highly adaptable and capable of reorganizing itself in response to learning and experience, a phenomenon known as neuroplasticity. When explicit instruction is provided, particularly in structured and systematic ways, it can capitalize on the brain's ability to rewire neural connections and strengthen pathways associated with new knowledge and skills.

2. Mirror Neurons and Social Learning: Mirror neurons are a type of brain cell that fires both when an individual performs an action and when they observe someone else performing the same action. This suggests that the brain is wired for social learning and empathy, allowing individuals to understand and imitate the actions, intentions, and emotions of others. In the context of explicit instruction, mirror neurons may facilitate learning by enabling family members to observe and emulate the teacher or parent's demonstrations and behaviors during modeling and guided practice.

3. Observational Learning and Imitation: Mirror neurons play a crucial role in observational learning and imitation, processes that are central to explicit instruction. When family members observe the teacher or parent modeling a specific skill or strategy, mirror neurons may activate, allowing them to internalize and reproduce the observed behaviors more

effectively. This supports the idea that explicit instruction can leverage the brain's natural mechanisms for observational learning and imitation to enhance skill acquisition and mastery.

4. Feedback and Reinforcement: Neuroscience research highlights the importance of feedback and reinforcement in promoting learning and skill development. When family members receive constructive feedback and positive reinforcement during guided practice and independent practice stages of explicit instruction, it can activate reward pathways in the brain associated with motivation, attention, and reinforcement learning. This can strengthen neural connections associated with the learned skill or concept, making it more likely to be retained and applied in future contexts.

In summary, recent neuroscience findings, including research on mirror neurons, provide valuable insights into the cognitive and neural mechanisms underlying explicit instruction and its effectiveness in promoting learning and skill acquisition. By understanding how the brain learns and processes information, educators and parents can design instructional strategies that are grounded in neuroscience principles and tailored to support optimal learning outcomes for learners of all ages.

Chapter 21: What is a Strength-Based Approach?

I am a passionate advocate for an interest and strength-based approach that includes neurodiversity-affirming practices in parenting, teaching, and tutoring for family literacy and family math. This approach emphasizes recognizing and celebrating the diverse strengths, interests, and learning preferences of each individual.

Here's how to implement such an approach:

1. Observe, Identify, and Celebrate Individual Strengths:

- Encourage parents, teachers, and tutors to recognize and celebrate the unique strengths, talents, and interests of each family member, including neurodiverse learners.

- Help individuals identify their strengths and interests in literacy and math by providing opportunities for exploration, self-discovery, and reflection.

2. Personalized Learning Plans:

- Collaborate with parents, learners, and other stakeholders to develop personalized learning plans that leverage individual strengths and interests in family literacy and math activities.

- Tailor instruction and activities to accommodate diverse learning styles, preferences, and abilities, including visual, auditory, kinesthetic, and multisensory approaches.

3. Strength-Based Instruction:

- Emphasize a strength-based approach to instruction that builds on learners' existing knowledge, skills, and interests.

- Design literacy and math activities that tap into learners' strengths and passions, such as incorporating favorite books, hobbies, or real-world contexts into learning experiences.

4. Flexible and Inclusive Learning Environment:

- Create a flexible and inclusive learning environment that accommodates the diverse needs and preferences of all family members, including those with neurodiverse characteristics.

- Offer choices and alternatives for engaging in literacy and math activities, allowing individuals to select formats, materials, and approaches that align with their interests and abilities.

5. Promote Positive Self-Identity:

- Foster a positive self-identity and sense of belonging for neurodiverse learners by highlighting their unique strengths, contributions, and perspectives.

- Encourage family members to embrace their neurodiversity as a source of strength and resilience, rather than a deficit or limitation.

6. Neurodiversity-Affirming Language and Practices:

- Use neurodiversity-affirming language and practices that promote respect, acceptance, and inclusion of individuals with diverse neurological profiles.

- Avoid pathologizing language and stereotypes, and instead focus on promoting understanding, empathy, and empowerment.

7. Collaborative Problem-Solving:

- Engage in collaborative problem-solving and decision-making processes that involve input from all family members, including neurodiverse learners, in designing and implementing family literacy and math activities.

- Encourage open communication, active listening, and mutual respect among family members to foster a supportive and inclusive learning environment.

By adopting an interest and strength-based approach that incorporates neurodiversity-affirming practices in parenting, teaching, and tutoring for family literacy and family math, families can create a nurturing and empowering learning environment where all members can thrive, grow, and succeed.

Chapter 22: How can we get an Astronomical Learning Approach implemented in education?

———

I personally believe that the covid-19 pandemic has forever changed our american education outlook. We can no longer ignore the issues that were going on. I believe that as we collectively embark on this journey that we need to create an inclusive and equitable learning environment for all. My goal with this book is to emphasize the importance of family literacy with structured literacy and family math with number sense in fostering a neurodiversity-affirming future.

Neurodiversity is the recognition and celebration of the diverse range of neurological differences, or neurotypes, among individuals, including autism, ADHD, dyslexia, dyscalculia, and other learning and developmental differences. It is crucial that we embrace neurodiversity and empower all individuals, regardless of their neurological profile, to reach their full potential.

Family literacy and family math provide essential opportunities for individuals, including neurodiverse learners, to develop fundamental literacy and math skills that are vital for success in academic and everyday contexts. Structured literacy instruction offers explicit and systematic teaching of phonemic awareness, phonics, fluency, vocabulary, and comprehension skills, benefiting all learners, especially those who may require additional support and multisensory strategies.

Similarly, developing number sense lays the foundation for mathematical reasoning, problem-solving, and critical thinking skills. Family math activities that focus on number sense enable neurodiverse learners to understand numerical relationships, quantities, operations, and mathematical concepts in a supportive and nurturing environment.

It is imperative that parents, educators, and professionals actively engage in family literacy and math activities, fostering a culture of support, encouragement, and collaboration at home and in the community. By celebrating individual strengths, acknowledging progress, and promoting a growth mindset, we can empower neurodiverse learners to build confidence, self-esteem, and a positive self-identity as capable and competent individuals.

Furthermore, we must advocate for inclusive education policies, practices, and resources that support the diverse needs of neurodiverse learners in schools and communities. By prioritizing equity, accessibility, and accommodation, we can create a more inclusive, equitable, and neurodiversity-affirming future where all individuals are valued, respected, and supported in their learning journey.

We must STOP seclusion, exclusion, abuse, and ableist practices that are neurotypically centric in nature.

In closing, let us unite in our commitment to foster a neurodiversity-affirming future through family literacy with structured literacy and family math with number sense. Together, we can make a positive difference in the lives of neurodiverse learners and their families, shaping a brighter and more inclusive tomorrow for all.

Thank you for your dedication to reading this book and advocacy in support of neurodiversity and inclusive education.

About the Author

Mrs. Deanna, known as Astronomical Tutor on Instagram, is a passionate advocate for inclusive education and empowerment through knowledge. Her journey as a parent, homeschool educator, virtual tutor, and now an author has been driven by a commitment to unlocking the full potential of every individual.

With her self-published book, Astronimical Learning, on family and community engagement, structured literacy, math instruction, with a strength-based approach, Mrs. Deanna offers a transformative perspective on education.

Embracing neurodiversity as a biological reality, she challenges the limitations of traditional education systems, advocating for tailored approaches that honor the unique strengths and abilities of each learner.

Through her work, Mrs. Deanna strives to create a world where education is not a one-size-fits-all model but a dynamic process that celebrates diversity and fosters growth. Follow her on Instagram as Astronomical Tutor to join the journey towards a more inclusive and empowering educational landscape.

Read more at https://sites.google.com/view/astronomicaltutor/home.